This Journal Belongs To:

_____

YEARLY *Overview*

January

_____
_____
_____
_____
_____
_____
_____

February

_____
_____
_____
_____
_____
_____
_____

March

_____
_____
_____
_____
_____
_____
_____

April

_____
_____
_____
_____
_____
_____

May

_____
_____
_____
_____
_____
_____

June

_____
_____
_____
_____
_____
_____

July

_____
_____
_____
_____
_____
_____
_____

August

_____
_____
_____
_____
_____
_____
_____

September

_____
_____
_____
_____
_____
_____
_____

October

_____
_____
_____
_____
_____
_____
_____

November

_____
_____
_____
_____
_____
_____
_____

December

_____
_____
_____
_____
_____
_____
_____

NOTES & REMINDERS:

Humanity RUNS ON Coffee

DATE

TO DO LIST:

PRIORITIES:

DATE

TO DO LIST:

PRIORITIES:

Coffee ON MY Mind

_____

_____

_____

_____

_____

_____

_____

_____

_____

_____

_____

_____

NOTES:

I LOVE YOU
~ *but* ~
first ¨
coffee

REMINDERS:

DATE

TO DO LIST:

PRIORITIES:

I am
gonna
be
strong
for
you

DATE

TO DO LIST:

PRIORITIES:

COFFEE,
please

DATE

TO DO LIST:

PRIORITIES:

GOOD
Vibes
AND
Coffee GOOD

DATE

_____

PRIORITIES:

PEACE LOVE AND COFFEE

DATE

TO DO LIST:

PRIORITIES:

coffee makes Everything Better

_____
_____
_____
_____
_____
_____
_____
_____
_____
_____
_____
_____
_____
_____
_____
_____

NOTES:

I LOVE YOU
but
first *coffee*

REMINDERS:

DATE

PRIORITIES:

NOTES & REMINDERS:

DATE

PRIORITIES:

TO DO LIST:

COFFEE, please

DATE

_____

PRIORITIES:

TO DO LIST:

☐
☐
☐
☐
☐
☐
☐
☐
☐
☐
☐
☐
☐
☐
☐

Let's have a
COFFEE
BREAK

DATE

TO DO LIST:

PRIORITIES:

_____
_____
_____
_____
_____
_____
_____
_____
_____
_____
_____
_____
_____
_____
_____
_____
_____
_____
_____
_____

NOTES & REMINDERS:

DATE

TO DO LIST:

PRIORITIES:

DATE

TO DO LIST:

PRIORITIES:

coffee makes everything better

Humanity
RUNS ON
Coffee

DATE

PRIORITIES:

TO DO LIST:

LIFE
begins
with
coffee

_____
_____
_____
_____
_____
_____
_____
_____
_____
_____
_____
_____
_____
_____
_____
_____
_____
_____
_____
_____

NOTES & REMINDERS:

DATE

TO DO LIST:

PRIORITIES:

hold me tighter

DATE

_____

TO DO LIST:

PRIORITIES:

It's
coffee
o'clock

DATE

TO DO LIST:

PRIORITIES:

XOXO,
YOUR
coffee

DATE

TO DO LIST:

PRIORITIES:

DATE

TO DO LIST:

PRIORITIES:

keep
CALM
and
DRINK
coffee

NOTES & REMINDERS:

_____

_____

_____

_____

_____

_____

_____

_____

_____

_____

_____

_____

_____

_____

_____

_____

_____

NOTES:

I LOVE YOU
but
first **coffee**

REMINDERS:

NOTES & REMINDERS:

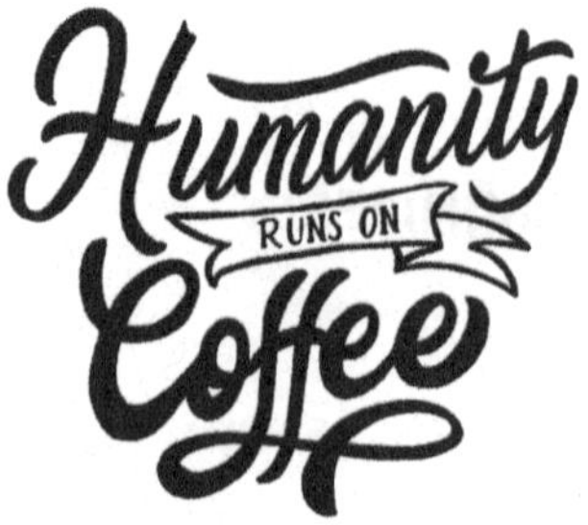

DATE

TO DO LIST:

PRIORITIES:

DATE

TO DO LIST:

PRIORITIES:

Coffee
ON MY
Mind

_____

_____

_____

_____

_____

_____

_____

_____

_____

_____

_____

_____

_____

_____

NOTES:

I LOVE YOU
~ *but* ~
first coffee

REMINDERS:

DATE

TO DO LIST:

PRIORITIES:

I am gonna be strong for you

DATE

TO DO LIST:

PRIORITIES:

COFFEE,
please

DATE

TO DO LIST:

PRIORITIES:

GOOD *Vibes* AND *Coffee* GOOD

DATE

PRIORITIES:

DATE

PRIORITIES:

TO DO LIST:

- [ ]
- [ ]
- [ ]
- [ ]
- [ ]
- [ ]
- [ ]
- [ ]
- [ ]
- [ ]
- [ ]
- [ ]
- [ ]
- [ ]

coffee makes Everything Better

_____

_____

_____

_____

_____

_____

_____

_____

_____

_____

_____

_____

_____

_____

_____

_____

NOTES:

I LOVE YOU
~ but ~
first ..
coffee

REMINDERS:

DATE

TO DO LIST:

PRIORITIES:

ENJOY
your
LIFE
with
COFFEE

_____

_____

_____

_____

_____

_____

_____

_____

_____

_____

_____

_____

_____

NOTES & REMINDERS:

DATE

TO DO LIST:

PRIORITIES:

COFFEE,
please

DATE

TO DO LIST:

PRIORITIES:

Let's have a
COFFEE
BREAK

DATE

TO DO LIST:

PRIORITIES:

XOXO,
YOUR
coffee

_____
_____
_____
_____
_____
_____
_____
_____
_____
_____
_____
_____
_____
_____
_____
_____
_____
_____
_____
_____
_____

NOTES & REMINDERS:

DATE

TO DO LIST:

PRIORITIES:

DATE

TO DO LIST:

PRIORITIES:

NOTES & REMINDERS:

Humanity RUNS ON Coffee

DATE

TO DO LIST:

PRIORITIES:

_____

_____

_____

_____

_____

_____

_____

_____

_____

_____

_____

_____

_____

_____

_____

_____

_____

_____

NOTES & REMINDERS:

DATE

PRIORITIES:

TO DO LIST:

DATE

TO DO LIST:

PRIORITIES:

It's coffee o'clock

DATE

_____

TO DO LIST:

☐
☐
☐
☐
☐
☐
☐
☐
☐
☐
☐
☐
☐
☐
☐

PRIORITIES:

XOXO,
YOUR
coffee

DATE

PRIORITIES:

TO DO LIST:

DATE

TO DO LIST:

PRIORITIES:

keep
CALM
and
DRINK
coffee

_____
_____
_____
_____
_____
_____
_____
_____
_____
_____
_____
_____
_____
_____
_____
_____
_____
_____

NOTES & REMINDERS:

_____

_____

_____

_____

_____

_____

_____

_____

_____

_____

_____

_____

_____

_____

NOTES:

I LOVE YOU
but
first
coffee

REMINDERS:

_____

_____

_____

_____

_____

_____

_____

_____

_____

_____

_____

_____

_____

_____

NOTES & REMINDERS:

Humanity RUNS ON Coffee

DATE

TO DO LIST:

PRIORITIES:

DATE

PRIORITIES:

TO DO LIST:

Coffee
ON MY
Mind

_____

_____

_____

_____

_____

_____

_____

_____

_____

_____

_____

_____

_____

NOTES:

I LOVE YOU

but

first

coffee

REMINDERS:

DATE

PRIORITIES:

TO DO LIST:

I am gonna be strong for you

DATE

TO DO LIST:

PRIORITIES:

- [ ]
- [ ]
- [ ]
- [ ]
- [ ]
- [ ]
- [ ]
- [ ]
- [ ]
- [ ]
- [ ]
- [ ]
- [ ]
- [ ]
- [ ]

COFFEE,
please

DATE

TO DO LIST:

PRIORITIES:

GOOD Vibes AND GOOD Coffee

DATE

TO DO LIST:

PRIORITIES:

PEACE
LOVE AND
COFFEE

DATE

TO DO LIST:

PRIORITIES:

coffee makes Everything Better

NOTES:

I LOVE YOU
~ *but* ~
first
coffee

REMINDERS:

DATE

TO DO LIST:

PRIORITIES:

ENJOY your LIFE with COFFEE

NOTES & REMINDERS:

DATE

TO DO LIST:

PRIORITIES:

COFFEE,
please

DATE

TO DO LIST:

PRIORITIES:

Let's have a
COFFEE
BREAK

DATE

TO DO LIST:

PRIORITIES:

XOXO,
YOUR
coffee

NOTES & REMINDERS:

DATE

TO DO LIST:

PRIORITIES:

DATE

TO DO LIST:

PRIORITIES:

NOTES & REMINDERS:

Humanity RUNS ON Coffee

DATE

TO DO LIST:

PRIORITIES:

LIFE begins with coffee

_____

_____

_____

_____

_____

_____

_____

_____

_____

_____

_____

_____

_____

_____

_____

_____

_____

_____

_____

_____

_____

_____

NOTES & REMINDERS:

DATE

TO DO LIST:

PRIORITIES:

hold me tighter

DATE

TO DO LIST:

PRIORITIES:

It's coffee o'clock

DATE

PRIORITIES:

TO DO LIST:

XOXO,
YOUR
coffee

DATE

TO DO LIST:

PRIORITIES:

DATE

TO DO LIST:

PRIORITIES:

- [ ]
- [ ]
- [ ]
- [ ]
- [ ]
- [ ]
- [ ]
- [ ]
- [ ]
- [ ]
- [ ]
- [ ]
- [ ]
- [ ]
- [ ]
- [ ]

keep **CALM** *and* **DRINK** *coffee*

_____

_____

_____

_____

_____

_____

_____

_____

_____

_____

_____

_____

_____

_____

_____

_____

_____

_____

_____

NOTES & REMINDERS:

NOTES:

I LOVE YOU
~ *but* ~
first ••
coffee

REMINDERS:

NOTES & REMINDERS:

Humanity RUNS ON Coffee

DATE

TO DO LIST:

☐
☐
☐
☐
☐
☐
☐
☐
☐
☐
☐
☐
☐
☐
☐
☐

PRIORITIES:

DATE

PRIORITIES:

TO DO LIST:

Coffee ON MY Mind

NOTES:

I LOVE YOU
but
first
coffee

REMINDERS:

DATE

TO DO LIST:

PRIORITIES:

I am gonna be strong for you

DATE

TO DO LIST:

PRIORITIES:

COFFEE,
please

DATE

_____

PRIORITIES:

TO DO LIST:

DATE

PRIORITIES:

TO DO LIST:

DATE

TO DO LIST:

PRIORITIES:

coffee makes Everything Better

NOTES:

REMINDERS:

I LOVE YOU
~ *but* ~
first ::
coffee

DATE

TO DO LIST:

PRIORITIES:

ENJOY your LIFE with COFFEE

NOTES & REMINDERS:

DATE

TO DO LIST:

PRIORITIES:

COFFEE,
please

DATE

TO DO LIST:

PRIORITIES:

DATE

TO DO LIST:

PRIORITIES:

XOXO,
YOUR
coffee

NOTES & REMINDERS:

DATE

TO DO LIST:

PRIORITIES:

DATE

TO DO LIST:

PRIORITIES:

_____

_____

_____

_____

_____

_____

_____

_____

_____

_____

_____

_____

_____

NOTES & REMINDERS:

DATE

PRIORITIES:

TO DO LIST:

- [ ]
- [ ]
- [ ]
- [ ]
- [ ]
- [ ]
- [ ]
- [ ]
- [ ]
- [ ]
- [ ]
- [ ]
- [ ]
- [ ]

NOTES & REMINDERS:

life
HAPPENS
COFFEE
HELPS

DATE

TO DO LIST:

PRIORITIES:

hold me tighter

DATE

TO DO LIST:

PRIORITIES:

It's coffee o'clock

DATE

TO DO LIST:

PRIORITIES:

XOXO,
YOUR'
coffee

DATE

PRIORITIES:

TO DO LIST:

life
HAPPENS
COFFEE
HELPS

DATE

TO DO LIST:

PRIORITIES:

keep CALM and DRINK coffee

NOTES & REMINDERS:

life
HAPPENS
COFFEE
HELPS

NOTES:

REMINDERS:

I LOVE YOU ~ but ~ first coffee

_____

_____

_____

_____

_____

_____

_____

_____

_____

_____

_____

_____

_____

NOTES & REMINDERS:

DATE

TO DO LIST:

PRIORITIES:

- [ ]
- [ ]
- [ ]
- [ ]
- [ ]
- [ ]
- [ ]
- [ ]
- [ ]
- [ ]
- [ ]
- [ ]
- [ ]
- [ ]
- [ ]
- [ ]

DATE

TO DO LIST:

PRIORITIES:

Coffee ON MY Mind

_____

_____

_____

_____

_____

_____

_____

_____

_____

_____

_____

_____

_____

NOTES:

I LOVE YOU
~ but ~
first
coffee

REMINDERS:

DATE

TO DO LIST:

PRIORITIES:

I am gonna be strong for you

Made in the USA
Monee, IL
11 June 2022

97864606R00073